14
Scriptural Principles
for Daily Living Vol.
3

14
Scriptural Principles for Daily Living Vol. 3

"Your words are a flashlight to light the path ahead of me and keep me from stumbling." [Psalm 119:105 TLB]

Anthony Adefarakan

GLOEM, CANADA

CONTENTS

Dedication	1
Acknowledgement	2
Introduction	4
Principle #1 Training Before Power	7
Principle #2 Offering Confusing Praise	12
Principle #3 The Joyful Order	18
Principle #4 Humility	21

CONTENTS

Principle #5 | Determining Your Destination in Advance — 25

Principle #6 | The Faith that Works — 29

Principle #7 | Cure for the Incurable — 33

Principle #8 | The Peril of Mockery — 39

Principle #9 | Facts Do Not Set Free — 42

Principle #10 | Arise to Shine — 47

Principle #11 | Engaging the Power in the Name of Jesus — 51

Principle #12 | Your Best Gift — 56

Principle #13 | Don't Run Without Power — 60

CONTENTS

Principle #14 — Making the Right Choices — **63**

Conclusion — **67**

WHY YOU REALLY NEED JESUS! — **68**

PRAYER POINTS — **73**

BECOME A FINANCIAL PARTNER WITH JESUS — **75**

About the Author — **78**

Dedication

I dedicate this book to God Almighty for His goodness and faithfulness in making His Word available to me. All glory to His Holy Name.

Also to everyone desirous of a closer walk with God, living out His precepts on a daily basis, I am in agreement with you all and I decree that grace for a closer walk with God is coming upon you in Jesus' Name.

Acknowledgement

I sincerely acknowledge my Eternal Father, Who alone is the Source of all wisdom. He is the Author and Finisher of my faith and it is of His fullness that the contents of this book have been drawn.

Also, I want to profoundly appreciate my dear parents – Prince and Mrs. Timothy Adefarakan – for bringing me up in the way of the Lord and for instilling righteousness consciousness in me. The wonderful education foundation I was given, coupled with their constant encouragement has empowered me to reach heights that were once beyond my imagination.

My most special appreciation goes to my sweetheart, Abisolami; without her help and support, I would never have enjoyed the conducive atmosphere needed to publish this book. I appreciate your love, encouragement, and the support you give at all times. Thank you so much. I love you, my Baby!

And to all my mentors in Ministry, I appreciate you all. Your investments in my life are not in vain. May the Lord reward you all in Jesus' Name.

Introduction

Life on earth has been described as a form of pilgrimage with eternity as man's final destination.

1 Peter 2:11 TLB says:

"Dear brothers, you are only visitors here. Since your real home is in heaven, I beg you to keep away from the evil pleasures of this world; they are not for you, for they fight against your very souls."

And Hebrews 11:13 also says:

"These men of faith I have mentioned died without ever receiving all that God had promised them; but they saw it all awaiting them on ahead and were glad, for they agreed that this earth was not their real home but that they were just strangers visiting down here."

In the course of this brief earthly sojourn, we

are bound to face certain situations capable of generating questions like *'what step do I take?' 'where do I settle?' 'who do I marry?' 'will I be rich or poor?' 'how do I finance my projects?' 'how do I take good care of my family?' 'how do I know God's will for my life?'* just to mention a few. Usually, we find it difficult to provide correct answers to these questions due to our weak mortal nature.

However, there is a manual for this pilgrimage, which is the Word of God. The One Who designed this journey for us has put in the manual all we need to navigate our way successfully and to eventually end up on the glorious side of eternity when the pilgrimage is over. Little wonder David prayed in Psalm 119:19 – *"I am a stranger in the earth; hide not thy commandment from me".*

The principles presented in this Volume 3 are also Bible-based and will deliver results every time they are applied because the Word of God is forever settled in Heaven (Psalm 119:89).

I pray as you read on, God's grace to apply these principles will rest upon you in Jesus' Name.

Anthony Adefarakan.

Principle #1

Training Before Power

Hebrews 5:12-14 KJV says *"For when for the time ye ought to be teachers, ye have need that one teach you again which be the first principles of the oracles of God; and are become such as have need of milk, and not of strong meat. For every one that useth milk is unskilful in the word of righteousness: for he is a babe. But strong meat belongeth to them that are of full age, even those who by reason of use have their senses exercised to discern both good and evil."*

A powerful weapon in the hand of an untrained soldier is simply a disaster waiting to happen.

All believers are soldiers called and commissioned to engage in spiritual warfare. Christianity is simply warfare as the Kingdom of Heaven launches spiritual missiles against the kingdom of darkness in order to have the will of God established on the earth. Remember when Jesus was teaching His disciples to pray in Luke 11:2-4? He said *'thy will be done on earth as it is in heaven'*. Now the devil isn't just going to fold his hands while God's will gets done on the earth as it is in heaven; he's going to fight to oppose it. And that's where the warfare comes in.

Ephesians 6:10-18 KJV says *'Finally, my brethren, be strong in the Lord, and in the power of his might. Put on the whole armour of God, that ye may be able to stand against the wiles of the devil. For we wrestle not against flesh and blood, but against principalities, against powers, against the rulers of the darkness of this world, against spiritual wickedness in high places. Wherefore take unto you the whole armour of God, that ye may be able to withstand in the evil day, and having done all, to stand. Stand therefore, having your loins girt about with truth, and having on the breastplate of righteousness; And your feet shod with the preparation of the gospel of peace; Above all, taking the shield of faith, wherewith ye shall be able to quench all the fiery darts of the wicked. And take the helmet of salvation, and the sword of the Spirit, which is the word of God:*

Praying always with all prayer and supplication in the Spirit, and watching thereunto with all perseverance and supplication for all saints;'

As soldiers, we are to make sure he doesn't have his way in our lives and in the lives of others. So we put on our whole armour of God and engage him with our spiritual weapons. If you are a Christian, that's the battle you are called to fight and there is no way to avoid it. You are in it already.

But here is the good news, no believer is asked to fight in their own strength; we are called to fight using the Name of Jesus with the strength and power the Holy Spirit provides.

Luke 10:17-19 says *'And the seventy returned again with joy, saying, Lord, even the devils are subject unto us through thy name. And he said unto them, I beheld Satan as lightning fall from heaven. Behold, I give unto you power to tread on serpents and scorpions, and over all the power of the enemy: and nothing shall by any means hurt you.'*

However, that being said, the Captain of our salvation – our Lord Jesus Christ – expects us to be well trained before He can entrust us with these spiritual weapons. He doesn't want us to misuse them or worst still be unable to use them correctly. That's why He made His Word available to us in order to get the necessary training required to become good and skillful soldiers. The Word of God is the Sword of the Spirit. You must stay in the Word and learn how to apply it in real-life situations in order to develop your sword skills.

Don't just cry *'Lord, give me power'* also cry *'Lord, teach me how to handle your power'*, and engage the training His Word provides. With that,

He will be able to trust you with His Power. Get trained!

Principle #2

Offering Confusing Praise

2 Chronicles 20: 1-25 KJV says *"It came to pass after this also, that the children of Moab, and the children of Ammon, and with them other beside the Ammonites, came against Jehoshaphat to battle. Then there came some that told Jehoshaphat, saying, There cometh a great multitude against thee from beyond the sea on this side Syria; and, behold, they be in Hazazontamar, which is Engedi. And Jehoshaphat feared, and set himself to seek the LORD, and proclaimed a fast throughout all Judah. And Judah gathered themselves together, to ask help of the LORD: even out of all the cities of Judah they came to seek the LORD.*

And Jehoshaphat stood in the congregation of Judah and Jerusalem, in the house of the LORD, before the new court, And said, O LORD God of our fathers, art not thou God in heaven? and rulest not thou over all the kingdoms of the heathen? and in thine hand is there not power and might, so that none is able to withstand thee? Art not thou our God, who didst drive out the inhabitants of this land before thy people Israel, and gavest it to the seed of Abraham thy friend for ever? And they dwelt therein, and have built thee a sanctuary therein for thy name, saying, If, when evil cometh upon us, as the sword, judgment, or pestilence, or famine, we stand before this house, and in thy presence, (for thy name is in this house,) and cry unto thee in our affliction, then thou wilt hear and help. And now, behold, the children of Ammon and Moab and mount Seir, whom thou wouldest not let Israel invade, when they came out of the land of Egypt, but they turned from them, and destroyed them not; Behold, I say, how they reward us, to come to cast us out of thy possession, which thou hast given us to inherit. O our God, wilt thou not judge them? for we have no might against this great company that cometh against us; neither know we what to do: but our eyes are upon thee. And all Judah stood before the LORD, with their little ones, their wives, and their children.

Then upon Jahaziel the son of Zechariah, the son of Benaiah, the son of Jeiel, the son of Mattaniah, a Levite of the sons of Asaph, came the Spirit of the LORD in the midst of the congregation; And he said, Hearken ye, all Judah, and ye inhabitants of Jerusalem, and thou king Jehoshaphat, Thus saith the LORD unto you, Be not afraid nor dismayed by reason of this great multitude; for the battle is not yours, but God's. To morrow go ye down against them: behold, they come up by the cliff of Ziz; and ye shall find them at the end of the brook, before the wilderness of Jeruel. Ye shall not need to fight in this battle: set yourselves, stand ye still, and see the salvation of the LORD with you, O Judah and Jerusalem: fear not, nor be dismayed; to morrow go out against them: for the LORD will be with you.

And Jehoshaphat bowed his head with his face to the ground: and all Judah and the inhabitants of

Jerusalem fell before the LORD, worshipping the LORD. And the Levites, of the children of the Kohathites, and of the children of the Korhites, stood up to praise the LORD God of Israel with a loud voice on high.

And they rose early in the morning, and went forth into the wilderness of Tekoa: and as they went forth, Jehoshaphat stood and said, Hear me, O Judah, and ye inhabitants of Jerusalem; Believe in the LORD your God, so shall ye be established; believe his prophets, so shall ye prosper. And when he had consulted with the people, he appointed singers unto the LORD, and that should praise the beauty of holiness, as they went out before the army, and to say, Praise the LORD; for his mercy endureth for ever. And when they began to sing and to praise, the LORD set ambushments against the children of Ammon, Moab, and mount Seir, which were come against Judah; and they were smitten. For the children of Ammon and Moab stood up against the inhabitants of mount Seir, utterly to slay and destroy them: and when they had made an end of the inhabitants of Seir, every one helped to destroy another.

And when Judah came toward the watch tower in the wilderness, they looked unto the multitude, and, behold, they were dead bodies fallen to the earth, and none escaped. And when Jehoshaphat and his people came to take away the spoil of them, they found among them in abundance both riches with the dead bodies, and precious jewels, which they stripped off for themselves, more than they could carry away: and they were three days in gathering of the spoil, it was so much.'

Did you actually read from verses 1-25 or you just glanced through? If you didn't, I sincerely recommend you read the entire text. That's what happens when the devil expects you to complain or murmur but instead, you offer praises to God.

Praising God in the midst of your troubles implies at least three things;

- It confuses the devil and makes him look like a fool.
- God sees it as proof of your trust in Him.
- It is a clear sign of maturity. It shows you are really growing in grace.

If you have not overcome murmuring and complaining as a Christian, you are still carnal and the devil will not take you seriously.

When praises go up, God's blessings come down. Learn to send something up before expecting something to come down, especially when you desire a change of story.

Principle #3

The Joyful Order

Psalm 16:11 KJV says *"Thou wilt shew me the path of life: in thy presence is fulness of joy; at thy right hand there are pleasures for evermore."*

Joy has been defined as a feeling of great pleasure and happiness. And that is very true. It is inwardly stimulated and most times it comes as a result of a decision rather than an occurrence.

But to experience this Bible kind of joy, there is an order to follow. And there is a popular song children used to sing in Sunday School classes in those days that describes the right order if joy must be sustainably present in one's life. The song says:

J-O-Y is:

J- Jesus first

O- Others next and
Y- Yourself last.

Let's take the *'Jesus first'* part. If you put Jesus first in your life, you will never run out of joy because in His Presence there is fullness of joy (Psalm 16:11); and joy is also one of the fruits His Spirit produces in believers (Galatians 5:22).

Matthew 6:33 KJV says *'But seek ye first the kingdom of God, and his righteousness; and all these things shall be added unto you.'*

When you make the Kingdom of God and what He wants you to do your priority, He ensures all other things (including the level of joy you desire) are added to you. You can't be a man of God's Presence and not be joyful.

Secondly, that song says *'Others next'*. When you live your life as a blessing to others, there is a level of joy and fulfillment that money cannot buy that floods your soul. When you pray for others, counsel others, encourage others or simply help others, you are sowing seeds of joy. Newton's third law of motion states that action and reaction are equal and opposite. So there is no way you will bring joy into the lives of others and lack joy in your own life. It's a spiritual law. You reap what you sow. Galatians 6:7 KJV says *'Be not deceived; God is not mocked: for whatsoever a man soweth, that shall he also reap.'*

And thirdly it says *"Yourself last'.* The Bible says in Philippians 2:3 - *'Do nothing out of selfish ambition or empty pride, but in humility consider others more important than yourselves.'* When you choose to please God and others before yourself, you are beginning to learn the secret of constant joy. Someone said 'what you invest in others lives, what spend on yourself dies.'

Those are the factors you will need to embrace in order to remain joyful no matter what happens around you. If you maintain that order, you will never run out of joy.

Principle #4

Humility

James 4: 6, 10 NASB says *"But he gives a greater grace. Therefore it says, "God is opposed to the proud, but gives grace to the humble...Humble yourselves in the presence of the Lord, and he will exalt you."*

Humility is a modest or low view of one's own importance, and it is such a treasured virtue in God's sight. That text says God gives greater grace (unmerited favour) to the humble and to be humble is to be Christ-like. Philippians 2:5-11 describes how He emptied Himself of His status as God and took the form of a servant in order to fulfill His purpose of coming to the earth – salvation of sinners; and He gave an invitation to emulate His humility in Matthew 11:28-30. It says *'Come to Me, all who are weary and heavy-laden, and I will give you rest. Take My yoke upon you and learn from Me, for I am gentle and humble in heart, and you will find rest for your souls. For My yoke is easy and My burden is light.*

Look at the story of Naaman in 2Kings 5:1-19. He was a leper; and upon hearing that Elisha (the prophet) could heal him, he came to him seeking his intervention. But contrary to what he expected, Elisha gave him an instruction that felt so humiliating to him considering that he was a man of great status (the Captain of the host of Syria). Let's read verses 9-14 from KJV:

'So Naaman came with his horses and his chariots and stood at the doorway of the house of Elisha. Elisha sent a messenger to him, saying, "Go and wash in the Jordan seven times, and your flesh will be restored to you and you will be clean." But Naaman was furious and went away and said, "Behold, I thought, 'He will surely come out to me and stand and call on the name of the LORD his God, and wave his hand over the place and cure the leper.'

"Are not Abanah and Pharpar, the rivers of Damascus, better than all the waters of Israel? Could I not wash in them and be clean?" So he turned and went away in a rage. Then his servants came near and spoke to him and said, "My father, had the prophet told you to do some great thing, would you not have done it? How much more then, when he says to you, 'Wash, and be clean'?" So he went down and dipped himself seven times in the Jordan, according to the word of the man of God; and his flesh was restored like the flesh of a little child and he was clean.'

Naaman was so angry at what Elisha told him to do (bathing in the River Jordan) that he was about to go back to his station when his servants approached him and advised him to do what the man of God asked him to do (since all he wanted was just to be healed). Naaman was humble enough to consider what his servants told him; he did what the prophet told him to do and his skin was fully restored. The leprosy literally vanished. Thank God his pride didn't cost him his miracle.

Also, in 1 Samuel 9:1-10, despite the fact that

Saul was the tallest man in Israel during his time, he still stooped low to the extent of taking advice from one of his father's servants. And as a result, he met the prophet that the Lord had ordained to anoint him as the first king of Israel. He didn't miss his opportunity.

How do you relate with your subordinates? Be humble and hear them out; they may be the ones ordained by God to connect you to your next level in life as was the case of King Saul. Be wise!

Principle #5

Determining Your Destination in Advance

Deuteronomy 30:15-20 KJV says *"See, I have set before thee this day life and good, and death and evil; In that I command thee this day to love the LORD thy God, to walk in his ways, and to keep his commandments and his statutes and his judgments, that thou mayest live and multiply: and the LORD thy God shall bless thee in the land whither thou goest to possess it. But if thine heart turn away, so that thou wilt not hear, but shalt be drawn away, and worship other gods, and serve them; I denounce unto you this day, that ye shall surely perish, and that ye shall not prolong your days upon the land, whither thou passest over Jordan to go to possess it.*

I call heaven and earth to record this day against you, that I have set before you life and death, blessing and cursing: therefore choose life, that both thou and thy seed may live: That thou mayest love the LORD thy God, and that thou mayest obey his voice, and that thou mayest cleave unto him: for he is thy life, and the length of thy days: that thou mayest dwell in the land which the LORD sware unto thy fathers, to Abraham, to Isaac, and to Jacob, to give them."

Heaven is a destination, Hell is also a destination. Your arrival at either of the two depends on the road you choose to travel on, not when you are dead but while you are still alive. The road to Hell is very wide and accommodates any kind of life that agrees with your sinful inclinations.

Matthew 7:13 BSB says '...*For wide is the gate and broad is the way that leads to destruction, and many enter through it.*'

And Isaiah 5: 14 WBT says '*Therefore hell hath enlarged herself, and opened her mouth without measure: and their glory, and their multitude, and their pomp, and he that rejoiceth, shall descend into it.'*

To land in hell, all you need to do is to fully engage in all the sinful activities you can think of (without any form of repentance) and before you know it, you will be there. God forbid!

But to arrive in Heaven, JESUS is the ONLY WAY (John 14:6). You will have to *"Enter through the narrow gate..."* He said *'no man comes to the Father except by me'.*

To enter through this narrow gate, you will necessarily need to surrender your life to Jesus Christ and begin to follow His teachings as contained in the Bible. You can't obey some and ignore the others. It is a complete package. You will have to absolutely submit to His will and let Him have His way in your life and affairs. And considering the eternal benefits this attracts, He doesn't feel it's too much to ask. After all, He gave His own life completely according to the will of God in order to save mankind from the bondage of Satan and sin.

If you die now, where will you spend your eternity - Heaven or Hell? If you are not so sure about the answer, then there is still something to repent of. Go ahead and repent of that thing, Jesus is willing to forgive you and take you home at the end of your sojourn down here.

Choose your destination while you still have breath!

Principle #6

The Faith that Works

Galatians 5:6 KJV says *"For in Jesus Christ neither circumcision availeth any thing, nor uncircumcision; but faith which worketh by love."*

Ever wondered why some people exercise their faith for something and the thing doesn't happen? Well, maybe what makes faith work is absent.

Faith only works by LOVE! That is, the love question has to be answered before faith can be expected to deliver results.

The kind of love that gets faith to deliver results is not the one we just profess without deep-rooted conviction; rather, it's the type described in 1 Corinthians 13:1-13 NIV:

'If I speak in the tongues of men or of angels, but do not have love, I am only a resounding gong or a clanging cymbal. If I have the gift of prophecy and can fathom all mysteries and all knowledge, and if I have a faith that can move mountains, but do not have love, I am nothing. If I give all I possess to the poor and give over my body to hardship that I may boast, but do not have love, I gain nothing.

Love is patient, love is kind. It does not envy, it does not boast, it is not proud. It does not dishonor others, it is not self-seeking, it is not easily angered, it keeps no record of wrongs. Love does not delight in evil but rejoices with the truth. It always protects, always trusts, always hopes, always perseveres.

Love never fails. But where there are prophecies, they will cease; where there are tongues, they will be stilled; where there is knowledge, it will pass away. For we know in part and we prophesy in part, but when completeness comes, what is in part disappears. When I was a child, I talked like a child, I thought like a child, I reasoned like a child. When

I became a man, I put the ways of childhood behind me. For now we see only a reflection as in a mirror; then we shall see face to face. Now I know in part; then I shall know fully, even as I am fully known.

And now these three remain: faith, hope and love. But the greatest of these is love.'

Did you notice how that text started? It compared great manifestations of spiritual powers to mere noise-making if love is absent. And if you also paid close attention to how the text ended, 'love' was said to be greater than 'faith' and 'hope'. That is, no matter what you hope for or exercise your faith to receive, without love, they are exercises in futility.

God is love and all He does is based on His nature of love. So, to receive from Him, your faith must be accompanied by love; that way, you can be sure nothing will hinder the manifestation of your expectations.

Most of the miracles Jesus performed during

His earthly ministry were anchored on compassion (His love for people). He wasn't supposed to touch a leper as a consecrated Jew; but according to Matthew 8:1-3, He touched one out of compassion and healed him. Everything worked for Jesus because He did everything in love.

Don't just exercise faith or make prophetic confessions; also practice love. That's what gets the job done.

Principle #7

Cure for the Incurable

Isaiah 53:4-5 KJV says *"Surely he hath borne our griefs, and carried our sorrows: yet we did esteem him stricken, smitten of God, and afflicted. But he was wounded for our transgressions, he was bruised for our iniquities: the chastisement of our peace was upon him; and with his stripes we are healed."*

That's talking about Jesus; there is nothing called incurable with Him because His stripes can take care of any sickness or disease known to man or yet to be discovered.

Let me share this true-life story with you to

show how the incurable gets cured by His power. Several years ago, there was a certain woman who suffered a serious hemorrhagic condition. She bled so heavily that her case became a concern. It all happened that while she was growing up as a girl, she reached the age of puberty and started menstruating as it is normal with girls of her age. She would have her monthly period and after some days it would cease till the following month. She kept growing and going about her life as a normal person, full of dreams and aspirations. She worked so hard and became a woman of substance, having a great fortune. She could simply be described as rich and her life was going on beautifully well. However, a day came; she saw her menses (monthly discharge) and adjusted her body as usual to accommodate the blood flow for the few days it would run.

But to her surprise, the menses that had not taken more than 5 – 6 days before started extending. The blood flow continued for one week, two weeks, three weeks, four weeks, and was even entering the 12th week when she decided to seek medical assistance. And because she could afford it, she engaged the services of sound physicians. They ran several tests on her, after which they gave her some medications to help solve her problem. She took the drugs prescribed for her religiously with the hope of getting better, but to her surprise the bleeding got worse as the flow became heavier. Out of desperation, she decided to try other medical specialists who after several abortive efforts referred her to a Consultant Hematologist – who specializes in blood-related disorders.

At this time, her problem was no longer a matter of months but years. People had started avoiding her company; all her friends had deserted her because they just couldn't fathom what was responsible for her infirmity. She couldn't go about her business again because nobody was willing to transact any business with her due to the offensive odour emanating from her body. She was a complete mess and was merely living on the money she had managed to save while she was still healthy. On meeting this Consultant Haematologist, her hopes were so high that even when she discovered that his bill would cost her all she had left to live on, she didn't mind. She made all the money available to the man to commence treatment believing that once she became fine, she would work and earn money again. The Consultant commenced her treatment and displayed all his expertise acquired over the years. He did all he could but unfortunately, the woman's case got worsened. She was given a few more weeks to live as her continuous loss of blood would eventually terminate her life.

Disappointed, frustrated, and sad, this woman returned home and hopelessly retired to fate. "Come to think of it' she said, "I am alone in all this, no man will marry a bleeding woman, no company will employ a bleeding woman, socially I have become unacceptable, medical personnel has failed me, all my means of livelihood gone and I have been given few more weeks to live. Well, I will just sit down and wait for the inevitable death" she concluded.

It was now 12 good years that her blood had been flowing ceaselessly. One day, as she was still waiting for her final moment she heard of someone talking about a man named Jesus who recently drove out 6,000 demons from a mad man. She also heard that Jesus could heal any sickness and cure any disease. Upon hearing this, a little ray of hope rose within her. But then she heard that it was very difficult to reach Him because of the crowd who always go about with Him. At this point, she became sad again because she had lost so much blood and had become too weak to struggle with any crowd. Also, her smelling condition would not allow the multitude to be at home with her presence. But then she thought of something, she said: "I would try and go to this Jesus; I wouldn't struggle with the crowd, all I would do is just touch the hem of his clothes and I believe upon doing that, I will be well again". So she arose and went.

And true to the report she heard, a crowd was with Jesus; but she tried and made her way through to touch the hem of His clothes as she had purposed. And guess what? Immediately she did that, her 12 years of ceaseless bleeding which no medical expert could cure stopped, because power flowed from Jesus' garment into her body and she became fine right there with all her hopes, dreams, and aspirations restored. The power she contacted by touching Jesus not only healed her but also delivered her from death and gave her reasons to live again. Praise God.

This story was extracted from Mark 5:25-34 (**emphasis mine**). And the good news is this; the Jesus who attended to this woman is still alive today and forevermore with the same power and ability. (Heb13:8). Your own problem may not be related to bleeding; but remember, **He heals ALL sicknesses and cures ALL diseases.** Just go to Him like that woman and touch Him by faith, you will surely testify.

There are no incurable sicknesses and diseases when Jesus, the Great Physician, is involved. Withdraw the case from human clinics and place it in His Hands. You will surely testify. Try it, it works!

Principle #8

The Peril of Mockery

2 Kings 2:23-24 NASB says *"Then he went up from there to Bethel; and as he was going up by the way, young lads came out from the city and mocked him and said to him, "Go up, you baldhead; go up, you baldhead!" When he looked behind him and saw them, he cursed them in the name of the LORD. Then two female bears came out of the woods and tore up forty-two lads of their number."*

Mockery can be defined as teasing and contemptuous language or behavior directed at a particular person or thing. When you mock someone, you are actually insulting them and the consequences can sometimes be grievous as seen in the text above. Those children lost their lives because they mocked a man of God.

There is another story in the Bible that corroborates this assertion. It's in Genesis 19:12-25. The Lord had sent down His angels to Sodom and Gomorrah to destroy them because of their sins which He could no longer tolerate. But Lot and his family were living there, and they were righteous people so the Lord decided to show them mercy and take them out before raining down fire on them.

Still, in demonstration of the Lord's mercy to Lot, the angels asked him if he had anyone else they could rescue in that city, and he told them he had sons-in-law. So he went out to get them. Look at the response of the sons-in-law in Genesis 19:14 CEV;

'Lot went to the men who were engaged to his daughters and said, "Hurry up and get out of here! The LORD is going to destroy this city." But they thought he was joking, and they laughed at him.'

Instead of taking his words seriously, they laughed him to scorn and literally mocked him for what he said. They didn't realize that was their last and only chance to escape destruction. They didn't listen to their would-be father-in-law and they got burnt alongside others when the Lord rained fire down on their city.

That's another peril of mockery.

The Lord detests mockery. Proverbs 3:34 NLT says *'The LORD mocks the mockers but is gracious to the humble.'*

Those who mocked Elisha got destroyed by bears and those who mocked Lot's warning got burnt. Do not mock the Gospel of Jesus Christ, it is your last and only way out of eternal destruction!

Principle #9

Facts Do Not Set Free

John 8:31-32 GNT says *"So Jesus said to those who believed in him, "If you obey my teaching, you are really my disciples; you will know the truth, and the truth will set you free.""*

If the truth you claim to know hasn't been able to set you free, kindly drop it. What you have is a fact, and facts don't set free. If it is the truth, then you should be free.

There are several Biblical case studies when it comes to facts and truth. To help you understand the difference between them (facts and the truth), we will consider two major characters in the Bible -

Abraham and Sarah, according to Romans 4:17-21 KJV;

"(As it is written, I have made thee a father of many nations,) before him whom he believed, even God, who quickeneth the dead, and calleth those things which be not as though they were. Who against hope believed in hope, that he might become the father of many nations; according to that which was spoken, So shall thy seed be. And being not weak in faith, he considered not his own body now dead, when he was about an hundred years old, neither yet the deadness of Sara's womb: He staggered not at the promise of God through unbelief; but was strong in faith, giving glory to God; And being fully persuaded that, what he had promised, he was able also to perform."

It was a confirmed fact they could no longer bear children considering their ages. Abraham was 100 years old and his body was described as dead. Sarah was also 90 years old and her womb was described as completely dead. Biologists have this to say about menopause: *'Menopause is the time in a woman's life when her period stops. It usually occurs naturally, most often after age 45. Menopause happens because the woman's ovaries stop producing the hormones estrogen and progesterone. A woman has reached menopause when she has not had a period for one year.'*

Now, if we are to go by this definition of menopause, it means Sarah already lost her ability to conceive babies 45 years ago. As a matter of fact, at 90, she was already celebrating her 45th menopausal year anniversary. That is womb deadness in its raw form. Those conditions were real and they were established facts. Abraham and Sarah knew the fact about their conditions and everyone around them knew as well. They were no longer candidates for fruitfulness; no more babies – period!

However, they equally knew the truth about their conditions; so they decided to ignore the facts and embrace the truth.

What truth? The Lord had visited Abraham

and given him a promise of fruitfulness – Genesis 18:9-15. The Lord told him when he was 99 years old that his wife –Sarah – would give birth to a son the following year. That was a solemn promise from the One Who can never lie according to Numbers 23:19.

Abraham and Sarah ignored the deadness of their bodies and decided to hold onto God for the fulfillment of His promise by exercising an unwavering faith. And true to His promise, at 90 years of age, Sarah became a mother for the first time in her life (Genesis 21:1-8). She gave birth to Isaac.

Now, what set them free from their barrenness? The Facts? Not at all! It was the truth that set them free. *'Forever Oh Lord, thy word is settled in heaven'* (Psalm 119:89). When God says a thing, it must surely come to pass (regardless of how contrary things may look in the physical). He said *'So shall my word be that goeth forth out of my mouth: it shall not return unto me void, but it shall accomplish that which I please, and it shall prosper in the thing whereto I sent it'* – Isaiah 55:11.

Therefore, if you are interested in freedom from any kind of bondage – barrenness, sicknesses and diseases, demonic oppressions, depression, thoughts of suicide, bad habits, poverty etc, you need something more than the facts about your conditions as well as your doctor's prescriptions and suggestions. You need the truth. You need a Word.

And how do you get the kind of truth that sets free? SIMPLY OPEN YOUR BIBLE; THAT IS WHERE THEY ARE - John 8:32, John 17:17.

Principle #10

Arise to Shine

Isaiah 60: 1-3 KJV says *"Arise, shine; for thy light is come, and the glory of the LORD is risen upon thee. For, behold, the darkness shall cover the earth, and gross darkness the people: but the LORD shall arise upon thee, and his glory shall be seen upon thee. And the Gentiles shall come to thy light, and kings to the brightness of thy rising."*

'Arise, shine for your light is come and the glory of the Lord is risen upon you...'

Take note of the order in this scripture: until you **arise** your **shining** is not in view. What then does 'arise' mean? Well, it could mean different things depending on the context in which it is being used. For instance, to someone sitting or lying down, arise would mean stand up or get up. While to someone who is depressed or despondent, arise would mean come out of that state. And to the lazy or indolent, arise would mean get busy or do something. I could go on and on. But note this, whenever the word 'arise' is used, there are two things you should quickly consider – 'from what or where' and 'into what or where'?

Every time someone arises, they are arising from somewhere or something into somewhere or something. Jesus told the man he healed at the pool of Bethesda in John 5:8 KJV, *'...Rise, take up thy bed, and walk.'* This man had been lying down for 38 years due to his illness and when Jesus met him, he changed his position from lying down to walking. So, when Jesus said 'rise and walk', he arose from 'lying down' into 'walking'. That is how the word 'arise' works.

Now back to our text (Isaiah 60), it says 'Arise, shine'. It means if you must arise into shining, you have to arise from some things that are capable of preventing your shining. And these things include sin, previous disappointments, failures, discouragement, mistakes, broken relationship, sexual abuse, depression, despondency, drunkenness, drug abuse, illegal businesses, blackmailing, low self-esteem, inferiority complex, low IQ, laziness, mediocrity, multiple sex partners, shyness, unhealthy thoughts, secret societies (cults), cybercrimes and every other thing that has happened to you or that you are currently ashamed of.

You must arise from your past mistakes if you must shine. Isaiah 43:18-19 KJV says *'Remember ye not the former things, neither consider the things of old. Behold, I will do a new thing; now it shall spring forth; shall ye not know it? I will even make a way in the wilderness, and rivers in the desert.'*

To shine in this life that the Lord has graciously carved out for you, you must forget about your past and press towards your glorious future.

Also, you must arise from your sinful lifestyle if you must experience your shining. Sin and all your carnal inclinations belong to the darkness. And if you are part of the darkness, you cannot shine. You will need to belong to the light to be able to shine.

Ephesian 5:11 GNT says *'Have nothing to do with the worthless things that people do, things that belong to the darkness. Instead, bring them out to the light.'* So, do you really want to shine? Then, ARISE!

Principle #11

Engaging the Power in the Name of Jesus

Acts 3:1-10, 16 KJV says *"Now Peter and John went up together into the temple at the hour of prayer, being the ninth hour. And a certain man lame from his mother's womb was carried, whom they laid daily at the gate of the temple which is called Beautiful, to ask alms of them that entered into the temple; Who seeing Peter and John about to go into the temple asked an alms. And Peter, fastening his eyes upon him with John, said, Look on us. And he gave heed unto them, expecting to receive something of them. Then Peter said, Silver and gold have I none; but such as I have give I thee: In the name of Jesus Christ of Nazareth rise up and walk. And he took him by the right hand, and lifted him up: and immediately his feet and ankle bones received strength. And he leaping up stood, and walked, and entered with them into the temple, walking, and leaping, and praising God. And all the people saw him walking and praising God: And they knew that it was he which sat for alms at the Beautiful gate of the temple: and they were filled with wonder and amazement at that which had happened unto him... And his name through faith in his name hath made this man strong, whom ye see and know: yea, the faith which is by him hath given him this perfect soundness in the presence of you all."*

There is still power in the Name of Jesus. There was a time the Lord appointed and sent out 70 of His followers to go preach in every city and place He would later be visiting. When they returned, they could not contain their joy because they saw situations responding to the Name of Jesus. They told Jesus in Luke 10:17 KJV '*...Lord, even the devils are subject unto us through thy name.*' They used the Name of Jesus to cast out devils and the devils had no option than to leave. They were so excited.

Also, in the text above, Jesus had already ascended back to Heaven when Peter and John decided to use His Name to heal a man who had never walked for over 40 years (Acts 4:22). The power in that Name made the man strong and his miracle attracted wonder and amazement (Acts 3:10).

At another time, Apostle Paul used the Name of Jesus to cast out an evil spirit from a girl according to Acts 16:16-18. The Name of Jesus is the Name above every other name and everything in heaven, on earth, and beneath the earth humbly respond to it. Philippians 2: 9-11 BSB says *'Therefore God exalted Him to the highest place and gave Him the name above all names, that at the name of Jesus every knee should bow, in heaven and on earth and under the earth, and every tongue confess that Jesus Christ is Lord, to the glory of God the Father.'*

There is something about that Name; it never fails. And if you are a believer, you have access to it. In John 14:13-14 KJV, Jesus said

'And whatsoever ye shall ask in my name, that will I do, that the Father may be glorified in the Son. If ye shall ask any thing in my name, I will do it.' That is so direct, and He is known to always keep His promises like when He died and came back to life (as promised). He further promised in John 16:24 that whatever we ask in His Name we will receive, that our joy may be full.

However, there is a warning here. As powerful as the Name of Jesus is, not everyone is permitted to use it. You must have a relationship with Jesus to be able to use His Name. Trying to use His Name without having any relationship with Him could be disastrous. In Acts 19:13-16, some vagabond Jews (exorcists) tried to cast out evil spirits using the Name of Jesus. The evil spirit they were trying to cast out on one occasion answered them and said *'Jesus I know, and Paul I know: but who are ye?'* Before they knew what was happening, the man in whom the evil spirit was pounced on them and dealt with them to the extent that they ran out of the place wounded and naked. Do not attempt to use the Name of Jesus if you do not have a relationship with Him.

And for those of us who have surrendered our lives to Him, we can just go ahead and use the authority of His Name by faith and we will be amazed at the results. There is still power in the Name of Jesus. Hallelujah!

Principle #12

Your Best Gift

Romans 12:1-2 TLB says *"And so, dear brothers, I plead with you to give your bodies to God. Let them be a living sacrifice, holy—the kind he can accept. When you think of what he has done for you, is this too much to ask? Don't copy the behavior and customs of this world, but be a new and different person with a fresh newness in all you do and think. Then you will learn from your own experience how his ways will really satisfy you."*

The Best gift you can give to Jesus Christ is not your gorgeous attire, beautifully prepared meals nor your fat offerings; a life totally dedicated and devoted to Him and to the course of His kingdom is what He craves the most and highly treasures.

And if you remember what He passed through for your sake, I do not think that is too much for you to offer Him.

Jesus gave up His comfort, He gave up His convenience, He gave up His status as God and came down to mingle with mere mortals, He walked about in harsh weathers looking for the lost sheep of Israel, He traveled in stormy seas, He was heavily criticized and slandered, He stayed awake to watch and pray while others were sleeping, He left His biological family to focus on seeking and saving sinners, He was tempted at all points, He was persecuted, He was beaten, He was wounded, He was falsely accused, He was made to wear a crown of thorns, He was made to carry a very heavy cross up a hill and He was crucified naked in public view.

Jesus had all the powers in heaven, on earth, and beneath the earth at His disposal, but He never used them to His own advantage. He could stop and destroy those who came to arrest Him yet He yielded Himself so that the work of salvation He came to establish could be thoroughly accomplished. He endured all these so that you and I could be free from the powers of Satan and sin.

Now, for this Jesus Who passed through all that just for you, is it too much to give up your drinking and smoking habits for His sake? Is it too much to give up your sexual sins and indulgence in pornography? Is it too much to give up your lying and cheating lifestyle? Is it too much to give up your pride, arrogance, and superiority complex? Is it too much to dedicate some moments of the day just to worship and thank Him? Is it too much to make out time every week to fellowship with Him in Church? Is it too much to begin to live a life of holiness for His sake every day of your life? Is it too much to tell others about His saving grace and to just let Him use you for His glory? Jesus Christ is not asking for too much. He is only saying, 'Because I gave Myself for you, please give yourself back to Me.' It is that simple. Just live your life in such a way that it will honour Him and bring glory to your Heavenly Father.

That is the Best Gift you can give to Him - the whole of you. Total surrender!

Principle #13

Don't Run Without Power

Acts 1:4-5, 8 KJV says *"And, being assembled together with them, commanded them that they should not depart from Jerusalem, but wait for the promise of the Father, which, saith he, ye have heard of me. For John truly baptized with water; but ye shall be baptized with the Holy Ghost not many days hence...But ye shall receive power, after that the Holy Ghost is come upon you: and ye shall be witnesses unto me both in Jerusalem, and in all Judaea, and in Samaria, and unto the uttermost part of the earth."*

Power is defined as the ability to do work. That is, work will not get done unless power is in place.

The Christian race is serious work. It is not a religion where all you do is practice some forms of rituals, do some recitations and say some documented prayers, etc. Far from it. To run this Christian race effectively, with all the spiritual battles going on in the heavenly places and with all the deceptions and distractions the devil has strategically placed in our ways right on this planet, power is highly needed.

To try to run this Heavenly race without power is simply suicidal. Look at what Jesus told His disciples when He was about to depart. He had been with them and everything had been fine so far. With His Presence, storms had been calmed, demons had been chased out of people, miraculous feeding of multitudes had taken place and the things that the power of God could accomplish had been witnessed first-hand. But it was time to go back to Heaven and He warned His disciples to not depart from Jerusalem (where they were waiting) until they received the power of God through the Baptism of the Holy Spirit.

Thank God they waited. The Power came and they literally turned the world upside down despite the fact that some of them were illiterates (Acts 2:1-4; Acts 4:13; Acts 17:6).

Don't ever try to run the Christian race with all it involves without drawing from the Power the Lord supplies through the Holy Spirit. It can be very frustrating.

If you are already getting tired running the race, it's pretty too early because it will only terminate at the Master's feet in Heaven. There is Someone Who can help you run without you getting tired because it will only cost His own energy and not yours. He is called The Holy Spirit. Subscribe to His ministry now and the entire story will change. He is very much willing to help if you allow Him.

So are you ready to fully face the race to your eternal destiny? Ask Jesus for the BAPTISM OF THE HOLY SPIRIT TODAY!

Principle #14

Making the Right Choices

Psalm 32:8 BSB says *"I will instruct you and teach you the way you should go; I will give you counsel and watch over you."*

Life is full of options: blessings or curses, progress or stagnation, promotion or demotion, grace or disgrace, prosperity or poverty, joy or sorrow, profit or loss, favour or disfavour, love or hatred, strength or weakness, life or death, eternal life with God or eternal death with the devil etc.

One thing is important to note though, as numerous as these options are, life doesn't force any of them on you; it is what you request, based on your actions, that informs what life hands out to you.

Take for instance, life doesn't decide when you die. However, there are certain actions you may take that will leave life with no other choice than to hand death over to you. Ezekiel 18:4 says the soul that sinneth shall die, it didn't mention your name or anybody's name; but if you choose to start committing sin, you have automatically subscribed to death whether you are aware of it or not. And it's just a matter of time, the death that comes as a result of sinning will locate you (unless you repent and obtain God's forgiveness).

Generally, as mentioned in our introduction, life on earth has been described as a form of pilgrimage (1 Peter 2:11, Hebrews 11:13) with eternity as man's final destination; and in the course of this brief earthly sojourn, man is bound to face certain situations capable of generating questions like *'what step do I take?' 'where do I settle?' 'who do I marry?' 'will I be rich or poor?' 'how do I finance my projects?' 'how do I take good care of my family?'*

'how do I know God's will for my life?' just to mention a few. Usually, we find it difficult to provide correct answers to these questions due to our weak mortal nature.

But thanks to God, there is a manual for this pilgrimage, which is the Word of God. The One Who designed this journey for us has put in the manual all we need to navigate our way successfully and to eventually end up on the glorious side of eternity when the pilgrimage is over. Little wonder David prayed in Psalm 119:19 KJV – *"I am a stranger in the earth; hide not thy commandment from me".*

We are never alone in our decision making moments; God has given us His Word and has even promised to instruct, guide, counsel and watch over us according to our opening text.

If you will be wise then, learn to think more about what the outcome of your intended action would be before taking such actions. Consider the various outcomes that your action could likely attract and prayerfully make informed decisions thereafter.

Starting point: Decide for Jesus, He will help you choose wisely in other matters (Matthew 6:33). Remember, your choice will either make you or mar you. And once your choice is made, the consequences are inevitable. Start making the right choices.

Conclusion

So far, the Lord has revealed some biblical principles to us. The purpose is not just to know, document, or preach them, rather they were revealed so that we can walk in them.

According to John 8:32, only the truth that is known sets free. So, go through these principles one by one and determine to build your Christian walk around them for a life of Kingdom impact here on earth.

Jesus said in John 13:17(NLT) - *"You know these things- now do them! That is the path of blessing."*

May the Lord release upon you and your entire household the grace to walk worthy of His calling upon your lives in Jesus' Name!

WHY YOU REALLY NEED JESUS!

You might have heard a lot of Preachers talk about the importance of surrendering one's life to Jesus and even the dangers of not doing so at one time or the other without you being really moved. But with these three (3) important reasons highlighted below, I strongly believe you will not need another sermon before deciding to yield to His saving grace regardless of your religious beliefs.

1. **You have an Enemy to overcome:** There is an adversary who is all out to steal from you, kill you and destroy you regardless of your level of education, moral uprightness, societal influence, or even religious beliefs. He is Devil by name (John 10:10, 1 Peter 5: 8), and he doesn't release any of

his captives until he completely destroys their souls in hell. The ONLY One Who can deliver you from his manipulations and also save your soul from him is Jesus Christ.

2. **You have an Appointment to keep:** Being alive and reading this implies you have a very important and inevitable appointment to keep. It is an appointment with death (Hebrews 9:27). Death is the sure end of all mortals (of which you are part), and to enable you to prepare for this appointment without fear of eternal damnation, you need Jesus. He is the ONLY One Who has power over death (Revelation 1:18).

3. **You have a Judge to face:** Upon departure from this earth, you will have to stand before a judgment throne to render an account of your earthly life (Hebrews 9:27, Romans 14:12). The outcome of this judgment is what will determine your eternal abode which will either be Heaven

or the Lake of fire. Interestingly, the Judge Who will preside over your case and also decide where you will spend your eternity is Jesus (John 5:21-30, 2 Timothy 4:1). I perceive you are thinking "is God not our Judge? Why Jesus?' Well, you are not wrong. But God the Father Himself is the One Who handed over all the judgment to His Son, Jesus Christ. Read verse 22 of that John chapter 5. So Jesus is the ONLY One Who has the power to either judge you guilty or guiltless in eternity.

Now that you know these, the wisest thing you can do for yourself is to quickly establish a relationship with Jesus, since you don't even know how close your appointment with death is. To do this, say this prayer aloud:

"Lord Jesus, I am a sinner and I cannot help myself. Wash me in your precious blood and make me a new creature. I open the door of my heart to you today, come into my life and become my Lord and Savior. Grant me the grace

to overcome the devil, prepare me for eternity and help me to escape the judgment reserved for sinners. Thank You Jesus for saving me. Amen."

Congratulations! You are now SAVED. Go and sin no more.

To learn more about your new relationship with Jesus, kindly send an Email to info@gloem.org or emancipation4souls@yahoo.com, we will send you material that will help you. You can also call, text, or send a WhatsApp message to +1 587 9735910 or +1 587 9695910 for further assistance.

And to learn more about God, His Word, and His plans for your life, kindly visit our Facebook page [***https://www.facebook.com/gloem.org***] for daily meditation in the Word of God (all year round) and our Blog page [***https://gloem.org/myblog***] for life-transforming publications.

You are also invited to listen to Freedom Podcast: The Official Weekly Podcast of Global Emancipation Ministries – Calgary via https://anchor.fm/gloem

All these great resources capable of developing your spiritual stamina will help you become an overcomer in life regardless of what comes your way.

PRAYER POINTS

1. Father, thank You for opening my eyes to the truths contained in this book.
2. Father, please cause every experience in my life to bring you glory.
3. I destroy everything contrary to my spiritual advancement in Jesus' Name.
4. God of all possibilities, please cause my grass to become green again.
5. From today, my expectations shall no longer be cut short in Jesus' Name.
6. Father, beginning from now, please release upon me and my household the ability to walk with you faithfully in the Name of Jesus.
7. Father, I thank You for answering all my prayers. Glory be to Your Holy Name. Hallelujah!

ANTHONY ADEFARAKAN

BECOME A FINANCIAL PARTNER WITH JESUS

At ***Global Emancipation Ministries - Calgary***, our mandate is ***to liberate men through the knowledge of the Truth*** and our mission statement is ***creating channels through which men can encounter the Truth - [Isaiah 61:1-3; John 8:32, 36; I Thessalonians 5:24].***

Our Ministerial Activities include Rural and Urban Evangelical Outreaches, Prison Evangelism, Hospital Ministrations, Mobilization for Missions Support, Teaching of the undiluted Word of God, Scripture-Based Seminars, Discipleship, Training of Field Missionaries and Empowerment of underprivileged ones among other Field Ministerial Tasks.

If you sense the Lord is calling you to reach out to the lost by engaging in any of these activities or by assisting those involved with your resources, please feel free to join us. Let us come together as we take the Gospel of our Lord Jesus Christ to the hurting and forgotten ones. [Mark 16:15-20].

Please join us in these kingdom projects by making your weekly, monthly, quarterly, or annual donations to Global Emancipation Ministries – Calgary.

You can visit the "GIVE" section on our website, www.gloem.org, to learn about the ways to give.

For acknowledgment, please advise your donations to us by email: info@gloem.org or emancipation4souls@yahoo.com, and kindly include your details i.e. name, address, email, and location. Alternatively, you can simply call +1 587 9735910 to do the same.

You can also volunteer your gifts and talents in the service of the Lord through our ministerial platforms regardless of your location. To get information on how to go about this, please visit www.gloem.org and contact us via email: info@gloem.org or emancipation4souls@yahoo.com.

God bless you.

About the Author

By the special grace of God, **Anthony O. Adefarakan** is the privileged President of **Global Emancipation Ministries - Calgary (GLOEM)** with headquarters in Canada, North America, and **Emancipating Truth Ministry International (ETMI)** with headquarters in Nigeria, West Africa.

The Lord called him into the field ministry in February 2008 with the mandate to liberate men through the knowledge of the Truth, and by December 2012 he was ordained and commissioned as the Pioneer Pastor – in – Charge of The Redeemed Christian Church of God, Revelation Parish, Shalom Area under Delta Province III, Nigeria where he served until 1st February 2015 when he officially handed over to a new Pastor in order to focus on his field ministry to which the Lord had earlier called him and for which the authority of the church had already prayed and released him to undertake.

On 29th September 2013, he was awarded a Post Graduate Diploma in Tent – Making Mission from the Redeemed Christian School of Missions, Nigeria (RECSOM, Asaba Campus) where he also had the privilege to train Pastors and Missionaries as a lecturer in 2017.

Since the commissioning of his field ministry in 2015 he has had the opportunity to lead his ministry officers to field ministrations in different Prisons, Hospitals, Orphanages, Rural communities, Camp settlements, Markets, Local churches among other places with great successes on all occasions – such as the salvation of sinners, healing of the sick, financial empowerment of mission churches, provision of relief materials to the poor, provision of medical services to the underprivileged, baptism in the Holy Ghost, deliverance from demonic oppression, the release of inmates just to mention a few - all to the glory of God Who alone is the Doer.

He is the author of other best-selling titles such as *The Law of Kinds, Learning From the Ants, The Immutability of God's Counsel, Surely there is an End, Life Applicable lessons from the Book of Ruth, One thing is Needful Weekly Devotional Guide, Life Applicable Revelations from God's Word* **(Volumes 1 and 2)** among others.

He is blissfully married to Ifeoluwa A. Adefarakan and their marriage is fruitful to the glory of God.

Jesus is his Message, Freedom is the Outcome! (Isaiah 61:1-3).

www.ingramcontent.com/pod-product-compliance
Lightning Source LLC
Chambersburg PA
CBHW021430070526
44577CB00001B/141